# Nathaniel English
## in
# The Life of a Panther

Written by Michelle Person

Illustrated by Kaustuv Brahmachari

# ACKNOWLEDGEMENTS

To all of my students, past, present, and future, always remember there is more to the story than what you see on the surface.
One only has to look.

"I'm home," shouted Nathaniel as the front door slammed behind him, and his book bag dropped on the floor. "I'm in the kitchen," yelled Mom. Nathaniel ran into the kitchen and pulled a chair up to the counter and snatched one of the apples his mom was cutting and quickly popped it into his mouth. "How did you know those were for you?" asked his mom with a smile. "I didn't," said Nathaniel. "I'm just really hungry," he said as he reached for another.

"Lucky for you I'm so insightful," said Mom as she reached over and playfully pushed his shoulder. "I knew you would be home soon and figured you would be hungry," said Mom as she finished cutting the last of the apple. "So tell me about your day. What made you so hungry that you had to come home and steal my apples?" "You know, it's not really stealing if you were cutting them for me Mom," said Nathaniel.

"School was fine. I overheard Mrs. Smith, the kindergarten teacher, and my teacher, Mrs. Mack, talking before school started. Mrs. Smith told Mrs. Mack she was feeling overwhelmed because her assistant was out for the next two weeks and she didn't have anyone to read stories to the kindergartners while she worked with small groups of kids at the learning table. So I asked Mrs. Mack if some of the fourth-graders could volunteer to go down and read to the kindergartners so Mrs. Smith would have help. Mrs. Mack loved the idea so much she is letting me pick the volunteers, which books we will read, and train the other kids."

"That's awesome," said Mom. "And the fact you are organizing the entire thing is impressive. I'm very proud of you. You're a regular Huey P. Newton," said Mom as she bent over to kiss his forehead before placing the knife she used to cut the apple in the sink. "Thanks, Mom," said Nathaniel as he bit into another apple slice, "but who is Huey P. Newton?"

"Huey P. Newton was a community leader and founder of the Black Panther Party.  I think I have a book about him upstairs," said Mom.  "I'll go get it." Nathaniel smiled. His mom had a ton of books, and she was always telling him about people, places, and things that no one in school ever mentioned. Nathaniel loved listening to her stories. Mom returned to the kitchen while Nathaniel was drinking his juice. She put the book down in front of Nathaniel and began to read.

FOR
SALE

"Huey P. Newton was born in Monroe, Louisiana, in 1942. He was the youngest of seven children. When Huey was three years old, Huey's dad, tired of the constant racist treatment Black people faced in the south, decided to move the family to Oakland, California, where there were better paying jobs and where he hoped he and his family would be treated better.

Huey was an intelligent child, but he did not like school. Huey was not a shy child and did not have a problem disagreeing with a teacher.  As a result, he often found himself in trouble.  Despite not having a positive relationship with most of his teachers, Huey graduated high school and went on to college earning his associates degree from Merritt College.

It was in college where he met Bobby Seale. Together with Bobby, Huey would create the Black Panther Party for Self Defense."

"The Black Panther Party," interrupted Nathaniel.  I've seen pictures of them.  They dressed in all black and wore funny hats."

"Berets," said Mom.

"Huh?" said Nathaniel.

"The small circular hat the Black Panthers wore," explained Mom.

"They were called berets."

"Oh," said Nathaniel.  "What did the Black Panthers do?" asked Nathaniel.

"Well," said Mom.  "Kind of the same type of thing you did today when you created the tutoring group for the kindergartners.  They tried to create solutions to problems they saw in their communities.  There was a school in Huey's community that did not have a stoplight in front of it.  The school was on a very busy street and sometimes cars would come down the street too fast and kids would get hit."

One of the first actions of the Black Panther Party was to have members outside the school every day at three o'clock to help direct traffic and keep the kids safe until the city agreed to put a light in front of the school."
"Cool," said Nathaniel.

FREE CLINIC
FREE CLINIC
Oakland Community
School

"That was just one program Huey helped organize.  He and his friend, Bobby, organized a free breakfast program for students, established free clinics, and even started a school."

"Two guys from Oakland did all that?" asked Nathaniel.

"They sure did," replied Mom.  "Why do you seem so surprised? You know I am always telling you that you can do anything you put your mind to."

"I know," said Nathaniel thoughtfully.

"I know that look," said Mom. "What are you thinking?" she asked.

"Well, I'm just wondering if maybe I should make the tutoring program permanent and not just for the next two weeks. Maybe it's something we could do for the rest of the school year."

"I think that is a great idea," said Mom. "If anyone can pull it off, you can."

"I'm going to call Tariq and see if he wants to help me plan it," said Nathaniel as he polished off the last apple and headed upstairs.

"The revolution has always been in the hands of the young," said Mom quietly as she watched him take the steps two at a time on his way to explain his idea to his friend. "Good job, son."

# Book in Review

1) Based on the information on page 1, why is Nathaniel's mom in the kitchen?
   a. She is washing the dishes.
   b. She is making Nathaniel a snack.
   c. She is getting ready to make dinner.
   d. She is waiting for a cake to bake.

2) This question has two parts. First, answer Part A. Then, answer Part B.

Part A
What does page 2 show about Nathaniel?
   a. His love of school
   b. His talkativeness
   c. His patience
   d. His helpful nature

Part B
Select one sentence from the story that supports the answer in Part A.
   a. "I'm very proud of you. You're a regular Huey P. Newton."
   b. "So I asked Mrs. Mack if some of the 4th graders could volunteer…"
   c. "I didn't", said Nathaniel. "I'm just really hungry."
   d. "I knew you'd be home soon and figured you would be hungry."

3) Which detail from page 9 explains what the Black Panthers did?
   a. "Kind of the same thing you did today when you created the tutoring group."
   b. "There was a school in Huey's community that did not have a stoplight…"
   c. "They tried to create solutions to problems they saw in their communities."
   d. "It was in college that he met Bobby Seale."

Answers: 1) B 2) D, B 3) C

# Text Connections

| Text to Self | Text to Text | Text to World |
| --- | --- | --- |
| This remind me of when I… | This reminds me of when I read… | This makes me think about…. |
|  |  |  |

# Journal Response

What I liked best: _______________________________

_______________________________________________

_______________________________________________

_______________________________________________

_______________________________________________

_______________________________________________

_______________________________________________

_______________________________________________

_______________________________________________

_______________________________________________

_______________________________________________

_______________________________________________

_______________________________

# Journal Response

I didn't like the part: _______________________________

___________________________________________________

___________________________________________________

___________________________________________________

___________________________________________________

___________________________________________________

___________________________________________________

___________________________________________________

___________________________________________________

___________________________________________________

___________________________________________________

___________________________________________________

___________________________________________________

_____________________________

# Journal Response

What I liked best: ______________________________

_______________________________________________

_______________________________________________

_______________________________________________

_______________________________________________

_______________________________________________

_______________________________________________

_______________________________________________

_______________________________________________

_______________________________________________

_______________________________________________

_______________________________________________

_______________________________________

# Journal Response

What I would have added to the story: ____________________________

# Journal Response

Summary: _______________________________

___________________________________________

___________________________________________

___________________________________________

___________________________________________

___________________________________________

___________________________________________

___________________________________________

___________________________________________

___________________________________________

___________________________________________

___________________________________________

___________________________________________

___________________________________________

___________________________________________

___________________________________________

___________________